You are Younger than a Star

Written by
Katherine Halligan

Illustrated by
Sophia O'Connor

DK

The world is a wondrous place...
...and you are the most amazing part of it!
Katherine Halligan

You are bigger than a bubble...
...you are smaller than a whale.

Bubbles are pockets of air that float just about anywhere — in water, other liquids, or even in the air! The bubbles in a whale's trail can be very large, but they weigh almost nothing.

The blue whale is the biggest animal on Earth. It's about as long as 26 of you lying end to end, and weighs about as much as 9,000 children!

You are big, and you are small.

You are taller than a toadstool...
...you are shorter than a mountain.

Toadstools come in many shapes and sizes. The tiniest toadstool is much shorter than your littlest fingernail. The biggest toadstool is half a metre tall – about the same as two newborn babies!

Mountains come in many sizes, but they are all very tall. The tallest mountain in the world is Mount Everest. It's so high that it would take around 7,700 children standing on each other's heads to be as tall!

You are tall, and you are short.

You are faster than a tortoise...

Tortoises are very slow. The top speed of the Galápagos tortoise is just 0.26 kilometres per hour (0.16 miles per hour), while most children can walk around 4-5 kilometres per hour (2-3 miles per hour).

Cheetahs can run up to 120 kilometres per hour (75 miles per hour) – faster than a speeding car! But they can only run this fast in short bursts, before they need to rest.

You are slower than a cheetah.

You are fast, and you are slow.

You are louder than lightning...

Lightning itself makes no noise when it flashes. The flash creates heat, hotter than the surface of the Sun!

...you are quieter than thunder.

You are loud, and you are quiet.

The heat created by the flash of lightning pushes the air outwards so fast that it makes a noise, which is thunder! A sharp crack means it's close; a low rumble means it's farther away... but either way, it's time to get to a safe spot quickly!

you are harder than water...

Water feels wonderfully soft on your skin when you are splashing in a bathtub or stream, and especially when you're swimming in the sea!

Diamonds are the hardest material found in nature, and most take billions of years to form underground. Ancient Greeks and Romans believed they were the tears of the gods or splinters from falling stars.

...you are softer than a diamond.

You are hard, and you are soft.

You are lighter than an elephant...

A fully grown male African bush elephant can weigh up to 6,100 kilograms (13,500 pounds) – that's about as much as four cars or 305 of you!

The fluffy seedheads (clocks) of a dandelion weigh almost nothing at all, and can travel long distances on the wind or on the wings of birds.

...you are heavier than a dandelion clock. You are light, and you are heavy.

You are drier than a river...

Most of the water we use comes from rivers. Rivers are key to our survival, but they make up just the tiniest part of all the water on Earth.

Rocks are made up of minerals, and actually can contain very tiny amounts of water – but you really can't get water from a stone! Humans are made up of around 70 per cent water, just like the Earth is.

...you are wetter than a rock.

You are dry, and you are wet.

You are narrower than a sequoia...

Sequoia trees are some of the largest trees on Earth. The widest is called General Sherman. It measures 11 metres (36.5 feet) across — that's wider than a standard football goal!

You are rougher than a manta ray...

Some rays, including the manta ray, are smooth as silk, while others are more sandpapery. There are hundreds of different kinds of these fish.

...you are smoother than a seahorse.

You are rough, and you are smooth.

Most seahorses are covered in tiny, spiny plates. This rough, bumpy skin helps them blend in with their surroundings and protects them from predators.

You are cooler than a volcano...

Lava from volcanoes can reach temperatures of up to 1,250 degrees Celsius (2,282 degrees Fahrenheit). Boiling water is 100 degrees Celsius (212 degrees Fahrenheit), so a volcano is really, really hot!

Snowflakes are made when water droplets freeze, forming jagged crystals of ice that fall from the sky. The way they form means no two snowflakes are exactly alike.

You are warmer than a snowflake (and just as unique)!

You are cool, and you are warm.

You are brighter than the Moon...

The Moon does not shine its own light. The glow of the Moon that we see is actually reflected light from the Sun. The Moon appears to change shape, depending on how much of the Sun's light is blocked by the shadow of the Earth.

We measure light in "lumens". The average lightbulb puts out about 800 lumens. The brightness of sunlight is tricky to measure, but it is roughly 36,000 trillion trillion lumens!

you are darker than the Sun.

You are bright, and you are dark.

You are rarer than a beetle...

There are just over 8 billion humans in the world today. Scientists believe that there are 300,000 to 400,000 species of beetle on our planet right now. There are so many that a queue of all the beetles would wrap around Earth more than 150 million times!

Rhinos are one of the rarest animals on Earth. The rarest rhino is the northern white rhino: there are just two left in the world, both female. Scientists have been working hard to increase rhino numbers. In 2023, the number of southern white rhinos increased for the first time since 2012.

...you are more visible than a rhino.

You are rare,
and you are visible.

You are simpler than a coral reef...
...you are more complex than a jellyfish.

Corals might look like rocks, but they are living creatures. The most complex and diverse habitats on Earth, coral reefs have been around for more than 400 million years — since long before the time of dinosaurs!

You are simple, and you are complex.

Jellyfish aren't actually fish, because unlike fish they don't have any bones. They also don't have brains, blood, or a heart! They are basically floating stomachs, with stinging tentacles to help them move and catch prey.

You are stronger than a breeze...

A breeze is a light wind created near the shore by the difference in temperature between the land and water. Cooling breezes usually blow in from seas or large lakes onto warm land.

Tornadoes are rotating columns of air, created by the energy from a thunderstorm. Blowing at up to 483 kilometres per hour (300 miles per hour), these dangerous winds can rip buildings apart and throw cars through the air!

You are more gentle than a tornado.

You are strong, and you are gentle.

You are busier than a sloth...

Sloths are very slow animals that spend most of their time hanging motionless from tree branches. It takes them a whole month to digest a leaf, and they make a slow journey to the forest floor just once a week – to poo!

...you are more still than a hummingbird.

You are busy, and you are still.

Hummingbirds are the tiniest birds in the world. They can hover like helicopters, and fly upside down and backwards. Their wings flap around 70 times per second and up to 200 times per second when diving downwards!

You are sillier than a shark...

Sharks appear serious because they don't blink. Some sharks can have more than 300 teeth at any one time, which may sound a bit scary, but nearly all shark species are actually very gentle.

Monkeys smile, laugh, play, and tickle each other, just like humans. Unlike humans, monkeys don't stop being silly because someone tells them to... they just keep monkeying around!

...you are more serious than a monkey.

You are silly, and you are serious.

You are more ordinary than a peacock...

Peacocks fan their tails to attract mates. The "eyes" on their beautiful blue-green tail feathers make them look scary to possible predators, which is useful as well as pretty.

...you are fancier than a toad. You are ordinary, and you are fancy.

Toads' bodies have plain colours and bumpy textures that mimic rocks, dirt, mud, and leaves. This helps them blend in with their surroundings and hide from predators.

You are older than a firefly...

Fireflies live around two months as adults. They are in their eggs about three weeks, and are larvae for around a year or two, for a total lifespan of around two years. The oldest humans have lived to around 120 years!

...you are younger than a star.

You are old, and you are young.

Our Sun is young for a star, at around 4.5 billion years old. Scientists think the oldest star in the Universe is around 14.5 billion years old.

You are big and small, tall and short, fast and slow, loud and quiet, hard

...cool and warm, bright and dark, rare and visible, simple and complex, strong

About the Author

Katherine Halligan grew up in California, USA, and has studied, worked, and travelled all over the world. She had a successful career in children's publishing, writing more than 200 books for children as an editor before turning to writing full time. She now lives in Ireland with her husband, two daughters, and Molly the dog. She loves exploring the natural world, and wrote this book as a celebration of its rich diversity.

About the Illustrator

Sophia O'Connor is an illustrator who lives in Cornwall in England. Since graduating from Kingston University, she has been bringing stories to life with her art. Sophia begins her artwork by hand, using ink, watercolour, and mixed media with tools such as bamboo to create bold marks and unique textures. When she's not in the studio, Sophia enjoys venturing the wild coasts and moorlands of Cornwall, finding inspiration all around her.

Written by Katherine Halligan
Illustrated by Sophia O'Connor

Project Editor Clare Lloyd
Senior Art Editor Charlotte Bull
Managing Editor Penny Smith
Managing Art Editor Anna Hall
Production Editor Becky Fallowfield
Production Controller Magdalena Bojko
Associate Publishing Director Francesca Young

First published in Great Britain in 2025 by
Dorling Kindersley Limited
20 Vauxhall Bridge Road,
London SW1V 2SA

The authorised representative in the EEA is
Dorling Kindersley Verlag GmbH. Arnulfstr.
124, 80636 Munich, Germany

Text copyright © Katherine Halligan, 2025
Artwork copyright © Sophia O'Connor, 2025
Layout and design copyright © 2025 Dorling Kindersley Limited
A Penguin Random House Company
10 9 8 7 6 5 4 3 2 1
001–342807–Oct/2025

All rights reserved.
No part of this publication may be reproduced, stored in or introduced into a retrieval system, or transmitted, in any form, or by any means (electronic, mechanical, photocopying, recording, or otherwise), without the prior written permission of the copyright owner. DK values and supports copyright. Thank you for respecting intellectual property laws by not reproducing, scanning or distributing any part of this publication by any means without permission. By purchasing an authorised edition, you are supporting writers and artists and enabling DK to continue to publish books that inform and inspire readers. No part of this publication may be used or reproduced in any manner for the purpose of training artificial intelligence technologies or systems. In accordance with Article 4(3) of the DSM Directive 2019/790, DK expressly reserves this work from the text and data mining exception.

A CIP catalogue record for this book
is available from the British Library.
ISBN: 978-0-2416-9452-7

Printed and bound in China

www.dk.com

MIX
Paper | Supporting
responsible forestry
FSC® C018179

This book was made with Forest Stewardship Council™ certified paper – one small step in DK's commitment to a sustainable future. Learn more at www.dk.com/uk/ information/sustainability